CONFEDERAPHOBIA

CONFEDERAPHOBIA

An American Epidemic

Paul C. Graham

Shotwell Publishing

Columbia, So. Carolina

Produced in the REPUBLIC OF SOUTH CAROLINA by

SHOTWELL PUBLISHING, LLC
Post Office Box 2592
Columbia, South Carolina 29202

www.ShotwellPublishing.com

Cover Design: Hazel's Dream / Boo Jackson TCB

ISBN-13: 978-1947660021
ISBN-10: 1947660020

10 9 8 7 6 5 4 3 2 1

CONTENTS

PREFACE

THE SMALL WORK WHICH FOLLOWS is the outgrowth of a paper I wrote in 2015 for *The Palmetto Partisan*, the journal of the South Carolina Division of the Sons of Confederate Veterans, and which bears the same name. It later appeared, in a slightly modified form, on the Abbeville Institute's blog.

At that time, the anti-Confederate sentiment in this country was certainly pathological but not as reckless and violent as it is today. I could not have imagined in the summer of 2015, even after seeing with my own eyes the hysteria here in South Carolina that lead to the unceremonious removal of the Confederate Battle Flag from our statehouse grounds, that I would live to see monuments to honourable and decent men like Jefferson Davis, P.G.T. Beauregard, and—worst of all—Robert E. Lee, taken down so callously as has occurred recently in New Orleans.

The Orwellian spectacle of masked men dismantling these sentinels that had stood watch over the legendary, indeed, iconic Southern city with snipers on the roofs and police officers harassing and intimidating those opposed to their removal is almost too much to fit in my head.

Shockingly, the removal of these monuments was hailed as a great moral achievement which struck a blow against "racism" and "white supremacy." When the final monument was dismantled and removed, the one which honoured General Robert E. Lee, the act was celebrated in the streets:

> Bystander Brittnie Grasmick danced to the Queen song "Another One Bites the Dust," calling that an appropriate selection for the occasion.
>
> One young man rode a unicycle, children drew chalk hearts in the street and some young women jumped rope. Others brought out lawn chairs to watch, entertained by a trumpeter who played "Dixie" — but in a minor key.[1]

I'm not saying that General Lee was a perfect man, but I do not think the famous assessment of President Dwight D. Eisenhower was far from the mark when he said:

> General Robert E. Lee was, in my estimation, one of the supremely gifted men produced by our Nation. He believed unswervingly in the Constitutional validity of his cause which until 1865 was still an arguable question in America; he was a poised and inspiring leader, true to the high trust reposed in him by millions of his fellow citizens; he was thoughtful yet demanding of his officers and men, forbearing

---

[1] Jesse J. Holland & Janet McConnaughey. "New Orleans removes Lee statue." AP, 20 May 2017.

with captured enemies but ingenious, unrelenting and personally courageous in battle, and never disheartened by a reverse or obstacle. Through all his many trials, he remained selfless almost to a fault and unfailing in his faith in God. Taken altogether, he was noble as a leader and as a man, and unsullied as I read the pages of our history.

From deep conviction, I simply say this: a nation of men of Lee's caliber would be unconquerable in spirit and soul. Indeed, to the degree that present-day American youth will strive to emulate his rare qualities, including his devotion to this land as revealed in his painstaking efforts to help heal the Nation's wounds once the bitter struggle was over, we, in our own time of danger in a divided world, will be strengthened and our love of freedom sustained.[2]

Being the charitable sort of fellow that I am, I feel compelled to give the mayor of New Orleans the benefit of the doubt. Perhaps he was not aware of the long-standing belief that Lee was a great *American* hero. Perhaps he merely needed to draw his own conclusion from a *careful examination of the historical record*—

---

[2] Dwight D. Eisenhower Presidential Library, "Dwight D. Eisenhower, Records as President, 1953-1961; White House Central Files, President's Personal File Series, Box 743, Folder: PPF 29-S Lee, General Robert E."

something I would expect of any leader of merit to do before violently uprooting items listed on the National Registry of Historic Places.

[As I write this, I imagine the follically challenged mayor in a red velvet smoking jacket and monogrammed slippers, pouring over Douglas Southall Freeman's multi-volume biography of Lee in an overstuffed leather chair; Chopin's *Nocturnes* playing softly in the background ...]

This, however, I believe would have led to a very different outcome. Either that, or the New Orleans mayor is a better judge of character than Eisenhower, Churchill, (Teddy) Roosevelt, Lord Acton, and many, many others.

This, of course, is absurd; yet here we are.

I have written this book for Southerners, specifically those Southerners who have been emotionally, physically, or psychologically impacted by the open hostility against them for standing up for the good name of their fathers and the symbols with which they have long been identified. I do not say this with the hope that others will not read it—I hope they do—only that this piece of information may help orient the reader, especially the non-Southern reader, to the material.

I do not claim any special insights into what follows. I have merely tried to place the question of Southern Identity within the linguistic and ideological context of the modern left[3]—the intellectual and spiritual heir of those meddlesome **Yankees** (defined below) against which our fathers fought so valiantly to separate—with regards to their **ideological** (Also defined below) understanding of race, gender, sexual orientation, *etc.*

I'm sure that many believers in and defenders of the ideological faith of the left (and in some cases, the right) will be quite unhappy with me for my heretical use of their words, arguments, slogans, observations, and techniques that have heretofore been so successful in their secular inquisition against thought criminals and

---

[3] Wikipedia (wikipedia.org) entries on Racism, Sexism, Privilege, and especially Homophobia have been *essential* to this project. Since these ideologies inform much of the ongoing "dialogue" regarding the South and Southern symbols, understanding the lingo is imperative, especially if you plan to adapt it for another purpose (which is what I do in this book).

I am also indebted to Caesar Lincoln's book *Homophobia: The Ultimate Guide* (Kindle, 2015) for providing a template for working out the categories employed in the chapter "What is Confederaphobia?" Mr. Lincoln's categories had a clarity that enabled me to categorically interpret almost every other article I read in preparation for this book--regardless of the article's topic. All other sources, which are not adaptations, can be found in the notes.

un-PC[4] cultural expressions, but that is the nature of the conflict in which I find myself.

This is not a defence of the South; I do not think she needs one. I have no interest in converting Yankees to the Southern understanding of Southern history, or arguing with Yankees who claim to know us better than we know ourselves, or even respond to any charges, criticisms, and/or condemnations directed at the South or its people, but they are perfectly welcomed to follow along if they like.

* * *

There are two words that occur throughout this work that need to be defined to lessen the possibility of any serious misunderstanding regarding the people and/or ideas of whom/of which I shall be critical.

The first is the word is **YANKEE.**

By Yankee, I do not mean "Northerner," although there are many Northerners who are Yankees.

By Yankee I mean quite specifically a group of people descended—in some cases by blood, in other cases by general

---

[4] *i.e.,* politically correct

disposition—from New England and who can be easily recognized (to borrow from Dr. Clyde Wilson's definition) "by their arrogance, hypocrisy, greed, lack of congeniality, and penchant for ordering other people around."[5] In this view, social justice warriors, equalitarians, cultural Marxists of all descriptions, and other ideologues (left or right) are *Yankees* regardless of their geographical origin.

Most Northerners are NOT Yankees, although they seem to be "thickest on the ground" up there.

The second word is **IDEOLOGY** and should inform the understanding of "ideology" in all its variations, e.g., "ideological," "ideologue," *etc*. One of the best definitions that I have come across, and the one which informs my use of the word(s) throughout this work, comes from Roger Scruton who defines "ideology" as follows:

> Any systematic and **all-embracing political doctrine**, which claims to give a **complete** and **universally applicable theory** of man and society, and to derive therefrom a **programme of political action**. An ideology in this sense seeks to **embrace everything** that is relevant to man's political condition, and to **issue doctrine** whenever doctrine

---

[5] Clyde Wilson. *The Yankee Problem* (Columbia SC: Shotwell Publishing, 2016).

would be influential in **forming or changing that condition.** [6]

Ideology is not, therefore, mere opinion or belief; it is, rather, the rejection of what is and what can be known by individual and collective historical experience in favor of an abstract theory that categorically explains both how and why things *must* be in order for the species to "progress," that is, conform to the tenants and expectations of the ideological program which has been designed to "fix" humanity.

Cultures are developed and grow organically. Ideologies are artificially created and enforced. They are, by their very nature, revolutionary and hostile to anyone or anything that may interfere with their social or political goals.

Ideology and culture cannot peacefully co-exist.

* * *

It is assumed that the reader of this book is doing so voluntarily and, therefore, has voluntarily assumed the risk of exposure to ideas

---

[6] Roger Scruton, "Ideology" in *The Palgrace Macmillan Dictionary of Political Thought*, 3rd ed. (Palgrave Macmillan, 2007), p 317. Emphasis mine. (Thank you, Dr. Carey Roberts, for bringing this definition to my attention.)

that may fall outside the realm of the currently accepted narrative. Please feel free to close the book at any time. If you are easily offended, dear reader, this is your trigger warning. This is not a safe space. You have been warned.

Before proceeding, I would like to thank and acknowledge my mentor and friend, Dr. Clyde Wilson, for pushing me to complete this project. It would *never* have been done without his oversight and gentle, yet firm insistence that it be finished.

I would also like to publicly acknowledge the ongoing and unfailing love and support of my beautiful bride, Suzette, who has always urged me to be *true* to my beliefs and to be *brave* when they have lead me into paths that I would have rather not trod. I dedicate this book to you, dear one …

Paul C. Graham
Old Granby, South Carolina
Summer 2017

INTRODUCTION

ON FRIDAY, 10 JUNE 2015, after a series of vitriolic, angry and hate-filled rallies, a press conference from South Carolina Governor Nimrata "Nikki" Haley, a legislative *coup d'état* comprising an overwhelming majority of the General Assembly, and the stroke of the governor's pen, the Confederate Battle Flag was removed from its place of honour at the Confederate Soldiers' Monument on the grounds of the South Carolina Statehouse.

The seat of government then held by Governor Haley and the General Assembly—the very same seat of authority that called on the men memorialised by the display to defend the State in the 1860s—abandoned their trust and allowed this insult and betrayal of these South Carolina soldiers and their families to occur. The insult was as palpable as it was personal. While these men served in the military of the Confederate States of America, they have long been legally recognised as American soldiers.[7]

Haley and her accomplices foolishly viewed their actions as a great victory against hatred and intolerance. They were not alone. It

---

[7] See Congressional Appropriation Act, FY 1901; US Public Law 38 (1906); US Public Law 810 (1929); US Public Law 85-425 (1958).

appears that some kind of miracle was expected to sweep the land once the flag in South Carolina was removed. In an article paradoxically named "The Science of Why Taking Down the Confederate Flag Matters," Brian Resnic, writing for *The Atlantic*, stated that

> When South Carolina Governor Nikki Haley signed a bill Thursday to remove the Confederate battle flag from the grounds of the statehouse, the move was *more than symbolic*. Flags hold a *psychic power* over people. When we see them, the ideas and groups they represent make a mark on our minds and can change our behavior. *When the flag near the South Carolina Legislature is taken down Friday, that power will be removed with it* ... [8]

There is now, ironically (and, sadly, quite predictably), more hate and more intolerance than there was before, only now it is unabashedly directed towards native Southerners, their ancestors, and anything associated with them.

The events leading up to this affair provided the perfect storm.

---

[8] Brian Resnic. "The Science of Why Taking Down the Confederate Flag Matters," *The Atlantic* (theatlantic.com) 10 July 2015, Emphasis added.

The *natural outrage and revulsion* accompanying the vicious and unprovoked murder of the parishioners of Mother Emanuel Church in Charleston, South Carolina, by Dylan Roof was quickly seized upon and exploited by those who have long desired to see this so-called "controversial" and "divisive" symbol removed from public sight.[9]

In less than a week, the issue surrounding the Confederate Battle Flag displayed in Columbia went from a state and local issue to a national issue to an international issue. People poured into the capital city from all over the world—protestors, political activists,

---

[9] The State of South Carolina had been under a "tourism boycott" by the NAACP since a compromise was reached in the SC General Assembly in 2000. This compromise removed a similar flag from the dome of the State Capitol building and placed a historically accurate flag at a historically significant place in order to make the flag's intended meaning completely clear.

The flag was there to memorialize the South Carolina soldiers of the 1860s, not to protest the Civil Rights movement of the 1960s—a charge which was made *ad nauseum* decades after the flag was erected on the dome of the State Capitol to commemorate the centennial of the "Civil War."

A monument to South Carolinians of African descent was erected on the grounds as part of that compromise. While this legislative action had the support of the SC Black Legislative Caucus, the NAACP broke ranks and had been doubling-down on the issue ever since. While there is too much to the story to include it here, it is important to understand the political context preceding the murders at Charleston.

and the media — most especially the media! There was little doubt by those of us who were there — the soldiers' flag was coming down!

After an 8,800% spike in sales of Confederate-themed merchandise on Amazon, they were banned. They were one of many retailers that joined in the purge. Others included Walmart, eBay, Sears, K-Mart, Etsy, Spencer's, Target, Google shopping, NASCAR, Overstock.com, Apple, and many, many more.

Things took a turn for the weird when Warner Brothers ended the production for the "General Lee," a toy replica of the 1969 Dodge Charger from the '70s television show "The Dukes of Hazzard."[10] They would later cease licensing any "Dukes" product which featured the flag. Television stations soon began cancelling re-runs of the Dukes. Them Dukes — those good ol' boys who never meant no harm — were done!

Then came government bans. Of special interest was the National Park Service which banned the sale of "stand-alone" Confederate-themed merchandise at Civil War battlefields and other relevant locations. From flags, to monument, to markers, to building and school names, to parks, bans began to take place at the state, local,

---

[10] For those that don't know, it wasn't the name of the car — and though this certainly didn't help matters — it was the "Rebel Flag" painted on the roof of the car that sparked the "outrage." I've seen replica models for sale since then, but they omit the flag on the roof ... Alas!

and national level. To this day the National Park Service continues this interdiction and there is no sign of the purge slowing or stopping.

While Dylan Roof was certainly enamoured with Southern symbols and imagery, his actions better resemble those of the Yankee terrorist John Brown than any actions attributed to Jefferson Davis or Robert E. Lee. In fact, Roof is the mirror image of Brown — both were fanatical ideologues; both wanted to incite a race war; and both were willing to shed innocent blood to accomplish their goals. Like Brown, Roof was ultimately a failure and, like Brown, he will, quite deservedly, be executed.

Dylan Roof is exactly what he was taught that he should be, not according to Southern history, tradition, or culture, but by public school textbooks, the mainstream media, and Hollywood propaganda.

Dylan Roof is every left-leaning pundit, politician, and political activist's wet dream. If he did not already exist, they would have had to invent him. Without him, the war on Southern history and symbols would have continued as it had for the previous fifteen years[11] — politically flaccid and morally impotent.

---

[11] *i.e.*, during the NAACP's economic boycott of South Carolina, 2000-2105.

Roof's story recurs over and over as a preface to every new outrage committed against the memory and symbols of the traditional South. Roof was and continues to be the *ultimate trigger object* evoked to incite hatred, fear, and demonization of the left's long-time enemy and largest stumbling block—the conservative South.

Perhaps if there was some consistency we could take their outrage seriously, but we can't.

The same people who flaunt Roof as "proof" of Southern racism and other moral deficiencies, continue to lecture us on being careful not to judge an entire group by the actions of an individual who may be linked to that group. Of course, we here refer to Islamic terrorism.

Why should Roof represent the cultural heritage of the South, past and present, when other mass murders of innocents, we are told, are *not* representative of their cultural heritage? There is no reason to flog a dead horse here. The hypocrisy is obvious and beyond dispute.

The ongoing use of Roof's crime to further a political narrative or to enact public policy is as dishonest as it is despicable.

* * *

The build up to and subsequent outcome of the 2016 presidential election, coming as it did on the heels of the great Confederate flag purge, did nothing to improve matters. The portrayal of Trump supporters as racist, ignorant, uneducated Bubbas was easily grafted upon the ongoing and increasingly hostile narrative of the South. As the reality of the outcome of presidential race began to sink in, things began to be not only more hysterical, but unpredictable and violent, as well.

Protests such as occurred at Berkeley, California, in April 2017 against Milo Yiannopoulos were an indication of where things would go. Were it not for his political views, Mr. Yiannopoulos would have been welcomed with open arms at Berkeley. If they are willing to riot, loot, and burn because they disagreed with the views of an open and flamboyant Jewish homosexual with a preference for black lovers, the radical response to the South was going to be ugly.

For those paying attention, it should have come as no surprise when Antifa and other violent radicals made their way to New Orleans.

AN AMERICAN EPIDEMIC

YANKEE TOURIST Lydia Folckomer of Brooklyn, New York, found herself in a real mess after she broke two miniature Confederate flags off a parked truck and ran away with them near the Battery in Charleston, South Carolina. Miss Folckomer, described in one report as an "actor, writer, producer and comedian" with "liberal sentiments,"[12] was arrested and charged with "malicious injury to real property." Why did she do it, you ask? According to officials, she grabbed the flags because "they upset her."

Miss Folckomer was arrested and spent the evening in jail. Her father Paul Folckomer was also arrested and spent the night in prison. He was charged with simple assault for blocking and grabbing James Bessenger, the chairman of the SC Secessionist Party, when Bessenger tried to chase his daughter down for stealing the flags.

Now, I don't fault a man for trying to protect his daughter, but if he would have instilled in her the fundamentals of good manners

---

[12] Sam Newhouse. "Brooklyn actress locked up for scuffle over Confederate flag in South Carolina," *Metro* (Metro.us), New York, 22 June 2016.

and a proper respect for other people's property, this would never have happened. But he didn't, and that's how it went down.

* * *

It seemed innocent enough. A toy subway car in Brooklyn's MTA shop, but this "Made in China" toy-was far from innocent. *Gothamist* reader Jim Lahey, sensing the urgency of the matter, sent photos in to the online news outlet. At first, there seemed to be nothing to these images — they looked like just a, well, toy. Upon closer inspection, however, it was clear that a message of hate had been sent to New York from the Orient. One of the cartoon passengers is not only a white male with sunglasses and a red bandana, he is also sporting a Confederate Flag T-Shirt!

The Gothamist quickly dispatched a team to the Transit Museum store at Grand Central Terminal to confirm this toy was the same one reported by Mr. Lahey, and lo and behold it was! With no warning labels or any indication of what lay inside, anyone could walk in and buy the toy for a mere $11.

How many were sold and how many were affected is unknown. We know of at least one patron who fell prey to this insidious act of aggression. In a tweet posted on this report, Raymar Hampshire, using the Twitter handle @Philanthroteer, wrote, "Um.. @MTA I bought your train toy for my nephew and discovered a man wearing a confederate flag.. (sic) do you support this?!"[13]

Thankfully word got out after the *Gothamist* broke the story and the news of the toy found its way into dozens of major and minor news outlets across the globe, including two UK and one Russian paper.[14]

One assumes that the foreign press cited references to the toy subway train so that any tourist to New York would not import the offending item back into their respective countries, but this is only speculation.

Once the MTA was finally contacted, they said it was actually the "crossroads of the world' design," *not* a Confederate flag.[15] While I seriously doubt this to be the case, dear reader, the design is slated to be changed so as not to unnecessarily upset, anger, offend, or confuse the good folks of New York.

---

[13] Jen Carlson. "This MTA Subway Train Toy Features a Confederate Flag," *Gothamist.com*, 21 March 2016.

[14] Google search, 15 June 2017.

[15] Alexandra Klausner. "MTA toy subway car appears to show image of commuter in Confederate flag shirt" *DailyMail.co.uk,* 24 March 2016

* * *

A "furious storm of confusion" rained down on the Indiana University campus at Bloomington (UI-B) when a tweet went out on what was otherwise an unremarkable spring evening. A man in white robes had been spotted — it appeared that a Klansman was on campus ... and he was carrying a whip!

"iu students be careful, there's someone walking around in kkk gear with a whip."

It took less than one minute for a concerned student tweet the disturbing news to the entire campus: "@IUBloomington there's a man walking around campus in a KKK hood carrying a whip and there's NOTHING you can do to make the students feel safe?"

Ethan Gill, being mindful of his responsibility as a resident assistant, sent out a Facebook post to the young scholars for whom was responsible. He was cautious, citing the First Amendment rights of Klansmen, but urged vigilance:

"...Please PLEASE PLEASE be careful out there tonight, always be with someone and if you have no dire reason to be out of the building, I would recommend staying indoors if you're alone. If you feel unsafe, please contact me..."

The feeling of safety was dwindling quickly and panic had begun to take hold ...

In an unrelated event on the campus of Bowling Green State University (BGSU) in Ohio, there was another Klan sighting. Unlike the sighting at UI-B the hooded miscreant—or miscreants—were not roaming the grounds, they were inside—apparently having a "Klan Rally" in one of the university's laboratories.

The student who happened upon the rally quickly took some video and sent it out *via* Twitter, taking special aim at University President Mary Ellen Mazey:

"There's been an ACTIVE KKK group in Bowling Green, OH since 1922. @PresidentMazy soo, how does this promote diversity &a *(sic)* inclusion??"

Being the presidential president that she is, President Mazey dispatched a university contingency to the scene. After a thorough investigation, the case was cracked.

Exercising a restraint that I could have never mustered, the president issued a response:

"Thanks for sharing, @autumpatrice. We looked into this. We discovered it's a cover on a piece of lab equipment..."[16]

Alas, no Klansmen on campus ... just some lab equipment, some protective covering, and a little student paranoia.

What about Indiana Klansman? Glad you asked...

There was no Klansman there either. Sadly, these young scholars could not differentiate between a Klansman with a whip (which did not exist) and a Dominican Monk in a traditional white robe with a Rosary (which did exist).[17] Alas!

* * *

It was their special day; their wedding day. The young couple did not go the traditional route, they wanted it to be an event to remember ...

---

[16] Emily Ferguson. "College Student Confuses Covered Lab Equipment With KKK Rally," The *Washington Free Beacon* (freebeacon.com), 24 January 2017.

[17] Griffin Leeds. "Everyone mistook a priest for a KKK member," *The Tab* (thetab.com), 05 April 2017.

They had met at a Civil War re-enactment, so a period wedding seemed perfect. The couple rented space at the Hotel Bethlehem in Pennsylvania for the occasion.

On the day of the wedding all was set — the cake, the flowers, and the *decorations*.

Guests began to arrive, some in period dress. It was sure to be a grand time for all, and it *almost* was, that is, until a passer-by glanced at the hotel's window and saw it — a Confederate flag!

Of course, "Old Glory" was also on display — this was a Civil War wedding after all — but it was the Confederate Battle Flag that transformed an otherwise decent and law-abiding citizen (one presumes) into a raging lunatic.

Upon viewing the object of offense, the unnamed man began "yelling loudly and shouting profanities in protest," even though the street was crowded and small children were present.

"He was freaking out, screaming and yelling," said police chief Mark DiLuzio. "He created a very aggressive and disorderly scene."

Traffic was blocked in both directions, reported one witness, as police intervened. When the officers arrived on the scene, the man continued to shout obscenities and would not comply with the instructions to stop. Ultimately, he had to be carried away. The offending display was later removed by the hotel.[18]

* * *

Just when you thought it was safe to visit the Battery in Charleston, South Carolina, without the fear of having a New Yorker vandalize your vehicle, a homegrown Yankee attacked a truck by ripping a $10.00 Confederate vanity plate from the front of the vehicle. Mt. Pleasant attorney Lee Anne Walters was apparently upset when she encountered SC Secessionist Party (SCSP) members "flagging"[19] near the scene of the crime.

According one source, "Following the incident, police arrested Walters—who was allegedly traveling with two children at the time—and charged her with damage to personal property and

----

[18] Pamela Sroka-Holzmann, "Man 'freaks out' over Confederate flag at Hotel Bethlehem, cops say." Bethlehem, PA: *Leigh Valley Live* (LeighValleyLive.com), 30 April 2017.

[19] A form of protest (or show of solidarity) in which people gather in targeted locations to carry/fly Confederate flag(s).

leaving the scene of an accident in which there was a personal injury."[20]

Wait! What? An accident?

Yep.

SCSP chairman James Bessenger described the encounter as follows:

> She was jeering at us as we were flagging the Battery . . . While jeering she nearly crashed her car. We laughed at her, so she got out of her car and ripped a (Confederate) flag off the front of Braxton's truck. I was trying to get a picture of her plate and car when she backed into me twice and left the scene.[21]

According to the police report—which was included in the article—Bessenger's "knee popped out of place and then back in as a result of the collision."[22]

---

[20] "Rebel Flag 'Hit And Run' Lands Lawyer In Hot Water," FITS News (fitsnews.com), 14 July 2017.

[21] *Ibid.*

[22] *Ibid.*

Not only is Ms. Walters facing criminal charges, she is also in danger of losing her license to practice law, bless her ...

* * *

It seemed like just another day at the University of Wisconsin-La Crosse (UW-L) for the vice chancellor of student affairs, Paula Knudson, until the phone calls, student visitors, and official "hate and bias" reports began to pour in.

A truck—a semi-tractor truck to be exact—had somehow breached the invisible line that marked the school's safe space and, without any apparent consideration for the students' feelings, was right there at the construction site at the student centre with a Confederate flag grill cover.

Shock waves spread as iPhones, Androids, and other electronic devises lit-up across campus warning fellow students about the hateful display.

After receiving the message loud and clear, "this is hurtful," Vice Chancellor Knudson called the university to action. Executive Director of Facilities Douglas Pearson was quickly dispatched to the construction site to get to the bottom of this blatant disregard for the emotional well-being of the UW-L's young scholars. Pearson spoke with the site supervisor, who in turn spoke to the truck driver, who in turn moved his truck "without complaint."

Among those who ratted-out the hapless trucker was physics senior Matthew Dreis, who saw the flag on his way to class Friday morning.

"That's very inappropriate," Dreis said. "I think we have problems with institutionalized racism at our school and when we see it at the construction site of the physical building where students are getting their education it solidifies that there's a problem with our campus atmosphere."[23]

It apparently never occurred to the future physicist that the truck had nothing to do with the school or, perhaps, that the trucker didn't view the flag in such terms. In fact, no thought seems to have been made of the trucker by anyone at the university — how *he was affected* by their hostility, inhospitality, and general lack of good manners.

In an email sent to students Friday afternoon, Vice Chancellor Knudson apologized for "the fear and angst caused by (the flag's) presence." She further explained that the flag-bespangled truck had been removed from campus.

* * *

---

[23] Jourdin Vivan. "UW-L discusses 'fear and angst' over Confederate Flag," *Lacrosse Tribune*. La Crosse, WI, 20 November 2015. (tinyurl.com/fear-and-angst)

Executives at ESPN, apparently worried that Asian-American Sportscaster Robert Lee would be mistaken for the former Commander of the Army of Northern Virginia, reassigned him from covering the University of Virginia's first football game of the 2017 season against William and Mary despite the fact that the general named Robert Lee has been dead for nearly 150 years. The game, held at Charlottesville, Virginia, had been the recent scene of a stand-off between Alt-Right and Alt-Left groups at the Robert E. Lee Statue that magically and without provocation erupted in violence.

It is not clear who or whom ESPN thought would be confused or upset by Robert Lee's appearance at the Charlottesville game.[24]

* * *

A student at Framingham State University (FSU), located 20 miles outside of Boston, was "traumatized" when a Confederate flag sticker was seen on another student's laptop computer.

This "bias incident" was quickly reported to FSU's "Bias Protocol and Response Team" who quickly responded to the complaint. FSU's "chief diversity and inclusion officer," Sean Huddleston,

---

[24] Matthew Haag. "ESPN Pulls Announcer Robert Lee From Virginia Game Because of His Name," *New York Times* (nytimes.com) 23 August 2017.

responded with a mass email to the student population, explaining the details of the incident and strongly suggested that those impacted by the incident seek counselling. The Bias Protocol and Response Team, said Huddleston, "will meet to determine any measures that may be needed to respond to this incident. Our primary goal continues to be to expeditiously address and resolve incidents that impede progress towards a welcoming and inclusive campus community."[25]

The irony of his position was apparently lost on Huddleston and other campus diversity enforcers. Some students, it is fair to say, are to be more "welcomed" and worthy of "inclusion" than others.

The traumatization of the "offending" student resulting from this hysteria is unlikely to be addressed. Rather, we expect this student received mandatory diversity and sensitivity training followed by a forced public apology and confession of his crimes before being expelled!

Unwelcomed, unwanted, a *persona non grata*, this young student is but one in a long list of causalities of the hatred and intolerance

---

[25] Brittney McNamara. "Confederate flag sparks controversy, conversation on Framingham State campus." *Metrowest Daily News*, Framingham, MA, 23 November 2015. (tinyurl.com/fsu-confederate-sticker)

characteristic of Confederaphobia, an epidemic that is sweeping America with new and increasingly outrageous manifestations.

WHAT IS CONFEDERAPHOBIA?

CONFEDERAPHOBIA IS CHARACTERIZED by an irrational and pathological hatred and fear of all things Confederate — flags, monuments, graves, portraits, trinkets, stickers, etc. — *anything* that could be associated, even tenuously, with the late Confederate States of America, including the region from which it sprang and those people and groups of people who are native or sympathetic to this region.

Confederaphobia expresses itself in many forms and should be explored in its various manifestations if we are to understand it.

Regardless of the shape it assumes, Confederaphobia has the characteristic of *dehumanizing* self-identified Southerners and seeks to *deny* them their humanity, their dignity, and their right to exist as they are — both individually and collectively — in the public sphere.

As a result, many Southerners hide in the shadows and talk in whispers, for fear of being outed. It's not that they believe that being Southern is wrong, although some certainly believe it to be a burden, rather it is the *fear of the repercussions* that they are likely to encounter if they dare act or speak *too* Southern; fear of being labelled as a "racist" or "white supremacist," for example, or stigmatized in other ways that call their character and reputation into question.

Because of their naturally good disposition, attention to manners, and desire to be left alone, self-identified Southerners are reluctant to make trouble, but the circumstances in which they find themselves are making this more and more difficult. Because of their strong attachment to family—which, for them is *intergenerational*—attacks on Confederate symbols are personal—attacks on family members and their own good name. The soldiers that have been memorialized in just about every city, town, hamlet, or cross-roads in the South, *are* family.

Even Southerners who are not fully conscious of these facts, or cannot fully articulate them, instinctively know that what is being done is *wrong* and they *resent* it.

It is important to state *emphatically* at the onset that being Southern or sympathetic to Southern history, heritage, and culture—including that of the Confederate era and symbols associated with it—is *not* wrong. Being moved at the sight of a Confederate Flag or the playing of "Dixie" is not wrong. Honouring the sacrifices of one's kith and kin of a bygone era is not wrong. Revering Confederate heroes like General Robert E. Lee and others is not wrong. T-shirts, belt-buckles, or any other item which exhibit the symbols of one's native region is not wrong.

What is wrong, clearly wrong, is being harassed, stereotyped, or insulted for being who and what one is—mentally, physically, or otherwise—in one's own country.

The problem is not with monuments and it is not with flags—inanimate objects which we may freely admit can be interpreted in

16

various ways—the problem is the *perception* that permeates almost every aspect of modern America—from schools, universities, the news media, the entertainment industry, and now even the mainstream churches.

The *problem*, dear reader, is *Confederaphobia*!

Throughout this section we will briefly look at various expressions of Confederaphobia as they relate to people, groups of people, as well as institutional and corporate entities.

Obviously, there is *much* overlap between these.

No person can truly be said to be an "individual" in the strict sense of the word, namely, unconnected from all others—an island unto himself, as the saying goes. Neither can groups, institutions, or corporate bodies be said to exist in their own right. They are created and maintained by people and do not exist in the abstract without them. Nevertheless, to focus in on these various ways of looking at humans and how they interact will be useful in describing Confederaphobia in a systematic way.

Internalized or Personal Confederaphobia

This aspect of Confederaphobia manifests itself in negative beliefs, stereotypes, stigmas, and/or prejudices against self-identified Southerners and traditional Southern symbols—that

Southerners are racist, redneck, or stupid,[26] for example. It is expressed by feelings of dislike, discomfort, disgust, fear, and/or outright hatred of all things Southern—especially anything that celebrates it as a legitimate inheritance or cultural identity. These feelings may be conscious or unconscious, but are increasingly more openly acknowledged and, strangely enough, celebrated.

Confederaphobia further manifests itself in behaviours which express a personal need to promote or conform to Confederaphobic cultural expectations. By expressing disapproval or hostility against people or things considered offensive, divisive, or racist, the Confederaphobe can identify himself as un-offensive, inclusive, and a friend of racial minorities, which may or may not be the case.

In many instances, the Confederaphobe is guilty of the characteristics he projects onto Southern people, and/or inanimate objects such as flags or monuments, and may serve as a way of coping with the inherent contradiction between his stated ideology

---

[26] These descriptive words were provided by Google's auto-fill function when I typed "All Southerners are" into their search engine. When I typed "Southerners are" I got the following: fake, stupid, rude, racist, lazy, dumb, backstabbers, backwards, evil, and idiots. The Google search engine appears to have Confederaphobic tendencies. Just sayin'…

and the reality of his own suppressed beliefs and tendencies; being dogmatic, hateful and/or intolerant, for example.

Because Confederaphobia has the effect of making the sufferer feel better about himself, any threat to the legitimacy of his position could have dire existential consequences and are, therefore, vigorously resisted.

Interpersonal or Social Confederaphobia

Interpersonal Confederaphobia is the outward or social manifestation of internalized or personal Confederaphobia. It is here that people interact, or avoid interaction; act, or avoid action in accordance with their beliefs and expectations. It is a means of objectifying and dehumanizing self-identified Southerners as well as solidifying the Confederaphobe's identity as "not them" — that he is neither a part of this group, nor is he sympathetic toward them.

The more subtle manifestation may include "redneck" jokes, name calling, stereotyping, and the like — all of which are discriminatory efforts at demeaning, ridiculing, and otherwise debasing self-identifying Southerners. More extreme manifestations of Confederaphobia, which are becoming more frequent, can result in various forms of "lashing out." Hatred and fear, coupled with a superiority complex and institutional approval fuels the expression of the more odious forms of Confederaphobia. In its most extreme expression Confederaphobia can lead to violence and/or murder.

More common, however, is the shaming of an "unenlightened" family member or friend, or "outing" a co-worker or colleague who identifies as Southern for the purpose of ridicule or retaliation.

Social Confederaphobia in Southerners is a bit more complex, and may be more destructive to both himself and others. Unlike the non-Southern Confederaphobe who "has no skin in the game," the anti-Confederate Southerner's resentment and/or rejection is set against his own family and cultural inheritance. While rooted in one or more of the Yankee ideological abstractions or *"isms"* — racism or sexism, for example — it is *more* than a *mere* ideological stance. (See "Born this Way")

Social Media

Social media has become a major platform for the expression of identity. While it has allowed many self-identifying Southerners to discover that they are not alone in their love for their traditional history, heritage, and culture, it has also exposed them to a level of hostility which would otherwise not have been possible. Things that one would normally keep to oneself — if not for the sake of common decency, the very real possibility that such talk might provoke an ass whuppin' — the anonymity in safety and issuing insults from a computer in the confines of one's home has emboldened even the most timid Confederaphobe.

A quick survey of some comments received on a fairly unremarkable Facebook post "shared" by yours truly provides an example of this behaviour:

"weirdo Confederate traitor"
"rednecks"
"booger eater"
"redneck scum"
"white supremacist"
"buffoons …"
"racist"
"ignorant"
"Good old boy Hicks drink shine and bullying gays and Blacks and Mexicans"
"complete idiots"

These, dear reader, are some of the more tame comments I received. The more profane entries have been omitted.

The point I am trying to make is that it is very unlikely that these comments would have been made to my face. In certain contexts, perhaps, but in normal, day-to-day interactions, it would be extremely rare.

It has been suggested that social media may help spread mass hysteria in ways previously unattainable in human history.[27] What was once limited to a relatively small group of people in a very

---

[27] See Laura Dimon "What Witchcraft is Facebook?" The Atlantic (theatlantic.com), 11 September 2013.

localised setting, now has the potential to trigger a global epidemic. Episodes of mass hysteria can now "spread and exacerbate" with social media "acting as the primary vector or agent of spread for this disorder."[28] In 2013, Robert Bartholomew, a New Zealand sociologist who had studied cases of mass hysteria for more than two decades, stated that epidemics spread by social media are "inevitable" and that "it's just a matter of time before we see outbreaks that are not just confined to a single school or factory or even a region, but covering disperse geographical area and causing real social and economic harm."[29]

I do not think it a stretch to state that we are now in the midst of such an episode. If you don't believe me, log onto Facebook, post a picture of Robert E. Lee, and say something positive about him.

Cultural Confederaphobia

Cultural Confederaphobia occurs when the norms and standards of "society" are arranged to systematically exclude the South as a legitimate and identifiable subgroup of the larger whole. This history, heritage, and cultural expression is deemed to be

---

[28] *Ibid.*

[29] *Ibid.*

aberrations from the norm, whether past or present. No part of the South's distinction from other national or sectional peculiarities is considered American—at least without the dubious characterization of being what is least desirable about it.

This is spelled out in detail through the various forms of media which bombards every aspect of our lives. This was once limited to print, television, and media, but we are now drip-fed this cultural poison from cyberspace through the constant barrage of news, entertainment, social media, and video games. When we are not asleep, we are checking emails, Twitter feeds, Facebook statuses, and the latest from our favourite blogs and news outlets.

When it comes to the South, there is the predicable cast of Southern stereotypes. Most Southerners, being good natured, laugh at these stereotypes. Few of us are uptight and are okay with laughing at some of our less-than-sophisticated peculiarities. Who doesn't, after all, love Jeff Foxworthy's "You might be a redneck if …" routine?

It is, however, one thing to joke and another thing to ridicule or demonize.

It is the latter that has taken the stage and screen in the past several years and shows a growing hostility towards the South and Southerners along with an overwhelming and unquestioning acceptance of cultural Confederaphobia.

* * *

The move towards contextualisation as a purported means of "preserving" (*i.e.*, not demolishing) Confederate and other "controversial" monuments and displays is one of the more recent attempts to impose Confederaphobia upon culture. It is a strange Orwellian assemblage of historical relativism and cultural imperialism which applies contemporary moral judgements and world views to those of the past. It is the opposite of what it claims to be. Contextualisation is really decontextualization — an attempt to explain away the plain and most obvious meaning of the display.

These displays are already contextualised. We know who erected these monuments, when they were erected, and why they were erected. If one wants to understand them, one may simply walk up to the monument and read the inscription.

If they were really monuments to "white supremacy" or some other nefarious cause, they would have said so during the unveiling ceremonies and inscribed them on the monuments themselves. Who would have stopped them, especially if the culture was as "racist" as these advocates of cultural genocide claim? The fact is that they did *not* wish to confuse anyone, they were perfectly forthright and clear so that they *would* be understood by future generations.

The purpose of contextualisation is not to contextualise at all — that is, to explain their *actual* historical context — but to demonise, ridicule, and imbue them with characteristics that the erectors of these monuments would have neither contemplated nor understood.

Institutional Confederaphobia

Confederaphobia is also outwardly expressed *via* the actions, attitudes, and/or policies of organisations such as governments, schools, colleges, corporations or businesses, chamber pots of commerce, and other entities that are hostile toward or discriminate against self-identifying Southerners. At the root of this collective expression is an adherence to "respectability" and desire to maintain the new American status quo. They have been so thoroughly indoctrinated (or bullied) that they have come to believe that their position is one of enlightened morality and cloaks itself, in many cases, in the language of patriotism (i.e., nationalism, Americanism, *etc.*) or, most recently, in the highly questionable language of "social justice."

Educational institutions—especially colleges and universities, but increasingly in K-12 public schools—which are permeated with strong ideological biases, have strictly implied rules or policies against any outward expression of one's Southern identity or views that fall outside of the accepted narratives of the South as racist, treasonous, and that the "Civil War" was all *about* slavery.[30] These

---

[30] While the topic of slavery and the War is outside of the parameters of this project, it is important. I recommend *Forced Into Glory: Abraham Lincoln's White Dream* by Lerone Bennett, Jr., an African-American scholar and historian, and executive editor of *Ebony* magazine for decades. Bennett is no fan of the Confederacy, but he gets Lincoln, slavery, and the War exactly right. If you are not interested in spending a lot of time on the topic,

self-identified Southerners are not allowed to form groups or clubs that would identify their cultural heritage as a component of its purpose or included in its activities.

Cultural reminders of the South, buildings named after noteworthy Southerners, statues, markers, and even personal displays of Confederate symbols (stickers, belt-buckles, or hanging a flag in a dorm room) are ridiculed at best, but, more often than not, banned.

Dissent from the ideological underpinning of Confederaphobic institutions are not debated, neither are they questioned. They are enforced!

* * *

The Confederaphobe is intolerant, hateful, self-righteous, and smug. He hates all those he deems hateful and does not tolerate those who he accuses of intolerance — with the exception, of course, of himself. The jaundiced eye through which he views the world in

———————————————

I wrote a short article entitled "How the War Was About Slavery" that sketches out the basic issues. You can access it at **tinyurl.com/graham-about-slavery**.

general, but the South in particular, is infected by ideological prejudice which he accepts absolutely and without qualification.

His world view is just as rigid and inflexible — indeed, dogmatic — as any religion which he is in the habit of condemning. He cannot and will not tolerate any deviation from his creed. Heresies, and the heretics who hold them, are sought out and made objects of derision; symbol and relics that do not conform to his world view are marked for destruction. He is a zealot in the very worst sense of the word.

He secretly revels in his moral and intellectual superiority and views himself as an enlightened and progressive being — thanking his would-be god (were he not an atheist) that he is not like the sinners he persecutes.

Hating those he claims hate, intolerant of those he claims to be intolerant, and imposing his world view through all available means at his disposal, he is the express image and likeness of the people he *says* he opposes. It is no wonder, therefore, that he comes unglued when he encounters anything which brings these suppressed characteristics to the surface. Removing "trigger" objects keeps his inner demons at bay.

This, however, is just a short-term fix.

If it were possible to eliminate all things Confederate from his view, he would simply turn his attention elsewhere. There is always another dragon that needs to be slain — something else that needs to be rooted out and destroyed in the name of the "ism" or "ology" *du jour*.

THE PATHOLOGY OF THE CONFEDERAPHOBE

THE CONFEDERAPHOBE, unlike other people who suffer from phobias, does not view his thoughts, actions, and/or behaviour as being abnormal. People with arachnophobia, for example, certainly hate and fear spiders, but they do not *blame* the spider for their malady. They know the *phobia is the problem*; that they, and not spiders or people who like (or at least tolerate) spiders, are "out of whack."

Imagine if they *did* blame spiders, advocated for the *extermination* of spiders, and were able to lobby public and private institutions or agitate in other ways to advance an anti-spider movement.

The very thought is both silly and absurd.

People suffering from arachnophobia do not see their reaction to spiders as virtuous, but rather for what it is, namely, an irrational fear that *can* and *should* be overcome so that a normal, happy, and productive life can be pursued. If successful, the arachnophobe can learn to manage his fears and find a way to live in a world where spiders exist. This will probably not include the adoption of a pet spider, or spending time watching spider documentaries on the National Geographic Channel, but he can certainly work towards finding a way to function and get along with the world as it is.

29

Confederaphobes *could*, if they choose to, learn to live in a world with self-identified Southerners and the traditional symbols, imagery, songs, *etc.*, that they love. They *could* even learn to be friends with them. This *cannot* happen, however, if he fails to see that the problem is in his *perception* and not the persons or objects of offense that torment him.

* * *

Unlike those who suffer from other phobias, the Confederaphobe has an elaborate justification for his pathological hatred and fear. These justifications are ideological—abstracted from rationalist axioms—which impose on him moral imperatives. Once internalized, an ideological template is created onto which all particulars *must conform*.

An example might be the belief that Southerners are racist. If this is the case, then any and all particular Southerners, by definition, must also be racist. Logically, it might be expressed in the following syllogism:

  1- All Southerners are racist.
  2- The author of *Confederaphobia* is Southern.
  3- Therefore, the author of *Confederaphobia* is racist.

If one believes (1) to be true and (2) to be true, there is no alternative but to conclude that (3) *must* also be true.

The construct of this belief is such that any/all particular Southerners must, as a logical necessity, have the universal characteristics of being racist (or choose any other stereotype to insert in its place).

If this is how you think, particular instances that seem to imply the existence of Southerners who do not have this/these trait(s) must be lying, delusional, speaking in a secret code language, or, if all else fails, are simply unaware of the racism (and/or other moral deformities) that afflict them. While logically consistent, this position dehumanizes and objectifies Southerners. Worse, it creates a scenario where nothing can count against the belief, <u>not even one's own experiences</u>.

What happens, for example, if one encounters a Southerner of African descent, proudly displaying a Confederate flag in his dorm room,[31] or opposing the removal of Confederate statues,[32] or joining a Southern heritage organization?[33] The Confederaphobe must (1),

---

[31] Byron Thomas of South Carolina in 2011. See **tinyurl.com/2011-Flag-Story**

[32] H.K. Edgerton, Gregory Newsome, Barbara Marthal, Anthony Hervey (killed in 2015) and Arlene Barnum, just to name a few.

[33] My Sons of Confederate Veterans Camp in Columbia, SC, recently inducted a gentleman of colour. He met the qualifications of membership — proof that he was descended from a Confederate Veteran —

deny the possibility of such a person, (2) ignore any evidence that might suggest such a possibility, or (3) destroy or discredit (1) and/or (2).[34]

Southern people who have been trying to show counterexamples to the Confederaphobic worldview are getting tired; they are growing weary of the bullying and harassment. They are coming to a realization that they are in danger—no longer figurative, but literally, and the time is coming when they will no longer be allowed to live peacefully if they fail to repudiate their Southern identity and denounce their Southern inheritance.

_____

and was welcomed like all other applicants of good character. It was not a big deal.

[34] _The Root_ (theroot.com) recently branded NBA legend Charles Barkley as a "black white supremacist," after his comments on crime and Confederate statues. I do not know what such an epitaph could possibly mean, but it is an excellent example of discrediting a person of colour for deviating from the narrative. See **tinyurl.com/barkley-bws**.

Confederate Reminders

REMINDERS ASSUME there is something in the person's experience to recall—a memory—but no living person has a memory of the Confederate era. These reminders—of slavery, for example—are not from experience; they are from instruction. It is, therefore, erroneous to say that Confederate symbols are a "reminder" of slavery and, for this reason, are offensive or upsetting. What is actually offensive and upsetting is what they were taught with regards to the symbols or objects. It is what they were taught, therefore, that triggers the emotional response to flags, monuments, street names, belt buckles, stickers, *etc.*, and not any so-called reminder.

This response is neither natural, nor inborn; it is a conditioned response. Confederaphobes have been conditioned to respond to Confederate or Southern imagery, in whatever form it may assume, with "moral" outrage which compels them to "take action."

The laboratory for this conditioning is the public school system—preschool/kindergarten through high school. The purpose, originally, was not to vilify the South *per se*, but to infuse the nationalist mythology of Abraham Lincoln and the characterization of America as a "NATION" dedicated to a "proposition," or at least this has been the case until very recently.

This view, which cannot stand up to historical scrutiny, stands in contradistinction to the principles and purposes of the War for American Independence and the subsequent UNION created through a voluntary compact between the states, first by the Articles of Confederation, and later by the U.S. Constitution. These States, sovereign and independent, after a long and bloody war with the British, were not going to set aside their hard-won status and join another highly-centralized regime, even one of their own making.

Such proposals were soundly rejected at both constitutional conventions and the ratifying conventions of the States that made the U.S. Constitution law.

There was no nation, no unitary and "indivisible" union, before the South surrendered in 1865 to the Northern combination of usurpers.

The government under which we are currently ruled has nothing to do with either the American War for Independence, or the ratification of the Constitution. The father of *this creature* is not the Virginia gentleman, George Washington, but the backwoods barbarian, Abraham Lincoln.

Washington, like Thomas Jefferson and other Southern statesmen, would have been Confederates just like their descendants were. For them, the Revolution and Constitution were not something about which you simply read in books, but were family legacies—events in which their fathers and grandfathers participated. Unfortunately, Washington and Jefferson now also being targeted by Confederaphobes and their strange assemblage of allies. They were Southern, after all ...

* * *

If the Southern view is a reasonable or legitimate point of view — one that cannot be simply dismissed out of hand — it must either be grafted onto the general narrative or it must be eradicated. Although it has not always been the case, over the past 50 years or so, the strategy has been eradication.

There was a time in the early to mid-20th century when it looked as though the long-standing breach would be healed and the sections could be reconciled — even happily reconciled — to their domestic partnership within the union, based on a national unity that included *mutual respect* for one another and a belief in the *sincerity* of conviction of both sides of the conflict, but that time has *long* passed.

The public schools now teach Southern children to be ashamed of who they are and others are taught to despise them. The full expression of this anti-Southern bias, up until recently, did not fully manifest itself until college. That is beginning to change with Common Core and other educational initiatives perpetrated by the federal government. Its purpose, it appears, is not to teach, but to traumatize, indoctrinate, and facilitate distrust between the races.

This educational "process" has the characteristics and the effects that have been associated with classical conditioning.

Dogs, in the case of Pavlov's famous experiments, salivate when a bell rings because they expect to be fed. These events have happened in conjunction so many times that the reaction seems "natural," that is, unconscious and automatic, through targeted manipulation.

The Confederaphobe is outraged or offended because he has been conditioned to associate the imagery of the South in general, and the old Confederacy in particular, with the imagery of American chattel slavery, Jim Crow, and the like.

This conditioning process is reinforced and emotionally charged through the news media and entertainment industry.

The news media presents the narrative and context through which we are expected to view *current* events. Stories are accepted or rejected insofar as they conform or fail to conform to the "appropriate" narrative.

The entertainment industry provides a narrative of *past events* through imagery, sound, and melodramatic story telling. This component is especially important in the conditioning process. It provides the *sensory and emotional content* from which one can draw as if it were one's own.

It's almost like being there, we say, but it's not. Rather, it is a short, controlled exposure to a time and place, presented from a particular point of view, and presented in such a way to maximize its emotional impact. Whether or not it conforms to the facts, television, movies, and other outlets inform what people *actually believe* to be the case.

The result is different for different people. Those that are non-native Southerners often respond with outrage and this expresses itself in hatred and fear. The self-aware Southerner — at least until he or she is exposed to their history — often reacts with guilt and shame. What they do with this guilt and shame depends on the individual.

As with all other threatening confrontations, the instinct of "fight or flight" comes into play — *fight* against what is said about one's people, or repudiate them and *fly* to the other side. Neither choice is a good one, and both are fraught with their own kinds of danger — dangers which are both *unnatural* and *unhealthy*.

Dogs are not naturally disposed to salivate at the ringing of a bell. People do not naturally overreact to history, symbols, or cultural heritage, whether it is one's own or that of another. It has to be taught and retaught until the narrative *appears to be self-evident* and the response *entirely appropriate*, even virtuous!

This can be undone — and Southerners have a better chance than most — but not without great personal effort and support from those who have travelled the path before. This, however, is rare.

Because Confederaphobia is sanctioned by the educational establishment and reinforced in the mainstream media, many decent people, regardless of their regional identity, are convinced that they are sufficiently educated on matters related to the South and its history. They are, therefore, immune to the effect of any evidence or argument that runs counter to their ideological beliefs regarding the South.

Contrarian evidence or argument is conveniently placed under the category "Lost Cause Mythology" or "Neo-Confederate Revisionism" by the court historians and their enablers. Once the label is affixed, there is no need for "educated" persons to consider the matter any further.

In far too many cases, this obstacle is insurmountable ...

THE CONFEDERATE FLAG
A SYMBOL OF HATE?

SYMBOLS ARE FUNNY things. They point beyond themselves to something else. Of what that "something else" consists is a matter of *interpretation*. A symbol's meaning cannot be fixed by definition; it must be interpreted. If it could be objectively defined, it would cease to be a symbol and become a *sign*. A red octagon with the words "STOP" at an intersection is not open to interpretation, neither is it a matter of opinion. It is also not a product of one's individual or collective experience. It means that one must STOP. You may not want to stop. You may not like stopping. You may even choose not to stop, but you know what the *sign* means — not just you, but all drivers.

The Confederate Battle Flag, Confederate monuments, and/or other Southern cultural expressions all can be interpreted as symbols of hate. They are certainly symbols that are hated by people for reasons that may or may not be merited ... but so what? Such is the nature of *symbols*.

The question is not whether the same symbol can mean different things to different people — experience clearly shows that it both can and does — but whether one group should be able to <u>dictate the meaning</u> of the symbol to another group of people.

The problem is not the symbol—the "thing" itself—it is in the mind of the thinker. The object hasn't the ability to offend, it merely exists. What one brings to the symbol determines how one interprets it; how it affects them. One has to be taught to interpret.

Had one never seen a Confederate Battle Flag or even heard of the South, one would feel nothing upon coming across one for the first time. Perhaps a sense of wonder or confusion might ensue, but there would certainly be no importation of political and ideological baggage to colour the response.

We bring the meaning to the symbol, alone it is nothing but an inanimate object.

It's one thing to acknowledge that the meaning of symbols is one of perspective, it's quite another thing to have the meaning dictated by ideologues who are not participants in the cultural tradition, or have removed themselves from it.

A symbol is not a sign.

One would not normally go to a rabbi, imam, or atheist to understand Christianity or Christian symbols. They certainly have opinions and beliefs, indeed, unique perspectives, about the Christian faith, but they are looking at it from the *outside*.

For them Christianity is not a living reality, but a topic of study.

Likewise, one might not get the best interpretation of the institution of marriage by visiting a women's shelter. You will certainly lean about a certain kind of marriage and the effects it can have in one's life, but these are exceptional cases. Certainly not marriage as is it is for most people, or marriage as it is intended to be.

Arguing from the hard case and choosing to maximize the significance of the aberration creates a skewed picture.

There are bad Christians. There are bad marriages. There are bad people.

This reality is not universal, it is particular.

Confusing the particular with the universal often gives undue weight to the exception. Once this occurs, stereotypes and generalizations take the place of experience, observation, and normal deliberation.

Southern symbols mean to the Southerner *exactly what they say that they do*. This does not mean that there cannot be alternative points of view, but rather that these explanations do not, cannot speak for those people for whom Southern identity is a *living reality*.

Those outside the fold are free to think and believe whatever they like, but let us not pretend that their interpretation can be *imposed* upon the culture from which these symbols spring and the people they represent. Their views may be interesting, and in some cases informative, but they are *not* authoritative.

The Curious Case of the Confederado

...the [Confederate] flag is a symbol of love — Bruno Lucke, age 9

In the months leading up to the 2016 Summer Olympic games in Rio de Janeiro, Brazil, journalist Martin Rogers made a truly amazing discovery. In the city of Santa Barbara D'Oeste, located about 335 miles west of the games, the unthinkable is not only thinkable, it is openly and lovingly embraced.

The Confederate Flag, described by Rogers as "the most controversial symbol in American history," flies without criticism or controversy. In fact, it appears almost everywhere and on almost everything—from belt buckles to bumper stickers. Children dress up in "Rebel" uniforms, Confederate graves are lovingly attended to by citizens, and the community gathers annually to celebrate their Confederate heritage.

Yes, that's right, dear reader ... Confederate heritage.

2016 marked the 150th anniversary of the arrival of the first Confederate settlers into this region. Ultimately about 30 families relocated to plant cotton or other agriculture commodities after the war. The lure of inexpensive, fertile land and the escape from the chaos inherent at the end of the war and the travails of Reconstruction proved to be more than enough motivation for theses former Confederates to strike out and start anew.

This anniversary was to be commemorated with a celebration "in a peaceful patch of leafy greenery next to a small chapel and near a graveyard where settlers and their descendants—Confederados as they are known here—have been buried for generations."

More than 2,000 people were expected to attend, including (gasp!) Brazilians of colour:

"Of course (black people) are welcomed," Kareline Townsend Lucke, says through a translator. "Welcomed in the best way possible like everyone, without any distinction ...."

In this alternative universe, Rogers astutely observed that there is no "negative association" with the flag that "many Americans see as a symbol of slavery and segregation." In fact, Rogers—despite his best efforts, I'm sure—could find no evidence of "racism." "Instead," noted Rogers, "they are proud of their culture, and Confederate memories are regarded as an appreciation of lineage, not a historical blight."

The words of Marcelo Sans Dodson, president of the Fraternidade Descendência Americana, sum up the problem as follows:

> The problem (in America) is not with the flag. The problem is with the people's mindset ....

> We are sad to see brothers and sisters in the U.S. fighting amongst each other and (not respecting) the right of one side to defend their heritage. That is the lesson that we here in Brazil have.

43

They should overcome and reconcile and make peace with each other and respect the right of fellow Americans to look at the Confederate flag with love....

Different people have different meanings. A good society is one that will respect (them).

In Brazil, Confederados do not suffer the ideological harassment and the political bullying that American "Confederados" do in the United States. Even this American journalist, despite his greatest efforts, begrudgingly acknowledged that there was nothing nefarious or hateful in the Confederados celebration of their history, heritage, and culture—including the so-called "most controversial symbol in American history," the Confederate flag—which is openly and proudly displayed as an emblem of their identity and a symbol of the love in the Brazilian city.

While Brazilian Confederados provide a compelling counterexample to the shallow and uncharitable treatment of Southerners expressing genuine affection for their history, heritage, and culture, I would not expect a reversal in the prevailing sentiment in the press.

Your Confederate Memorial Day observance or Living History event, dear reader, will not be covered with the same thoughtfulness and care. Brazilian Confederados can be taken at their word. American "Confederados" cannot.

EQUALITY & DIVERSITY
AMERICAN DOUBLETHINK

doublethink (dəbəl͵THiNGk/) *noun.* The acceptance of or mental capacity to accept contrary opinions or beliefs at the same time, especially as a result of political indoctrination.[35]

CONFEDERAPHOBES GIVE a lot of lip service to "EQUALITY." It is a moral imperative in which they all believe—or say they believe. One, however, finds it difficult to take them seriously. If people are, in fact, equal, then people ought to be the same, or at least similar, but there is a problem—DIVERSITY. Diversity is also a moral imperative. "Diversity," we are told, "is our greatest strength." If this is the case, it is not our "sameness" (equality) but our "differentness" (diversity) that is to be valued.

It is hard to imagine how these two beliefs can be true at one and the same time unless all our differences have equal value—that is, no cultural or ethnic distinction is better than the other; no moral or ethical system is superior to another, *etc.* One wonders how one can make any positive statement on how American society (if such a

---

[35] Term coined by George Orwell in his dystopian novel *Nineteen Eighty-Four.*

thing can be said to exist), or any society for that matter, should evolve or develop under these relativistic assumptions.

What are we to make of the moral posturing of those seeking to eradicate historical Confederate flags and monuments from the public sphere? Aren't they just another cultural expression, equal to other cultures, that diversity, our greatest strength, celebrates? I have never heard, "All people are equal, except …" or "Diversity is our greatest strength, unless …" but is this not the implication when it comes to Southern symbols? Does this not undercut their belief in both equality and diversity?

Culture/group X is not equal to culture/group Y. It is "bad" and, therefore, inferior, and, therefore, "unequal" to others.

Equality cannot be the belief in "sameness" or "equivalence" in either the case of individual or any given cultural expression. It can only be, if consistency and logic matter, *code language* of a privileged class who decide who is or is not to be included in this so-called "multi-cultural society."

There is *always* a group of folks with bad beliefs, or bad habits, or offensive characteristics that must be sacrificed for the sake of the greater good of the whole—a whole that by definition is EXCLUSIVE and UNEQUAL.

Today self-identified Southerners and their cultural markers are intolerable.

Tomorrow? Who knows?

BORN THIS WAY

IT IS NATURAL, normal, and healthy to embrace who and what you are. This is true for all people, including Southerners. Unless taught otherwise, the Southerner has no reason to think his genteel and easy-going ways are offensive; that he and his forebearers are "racist," or that his cultural heritage is an affront to common decency. It would certainly never occur to him that he should purposefully abandon his own cultural peculiarities for those of another.

Many people seem to believe that one can just move on from being Southern; that if these rednecks were just "properly" educated and taught the error of their ways, they could become *real* Americans.

To be Southern is not a choice, although the rejection of one's natural cultural and biological condition is. The rejection of one's Southern identity—whether by suppression or repression—often occurs after long-term exposure to Confederaphobic ideas and ideological constructs brought in from the outside. Although much of this occurs through various forms of media—television, news, and entertainment—the real psychological damage is done in the classroom. Confederaphobia is carefully inserted through mandatory attendance of public or government-licenced private K-12 schools before its full fury is thrust upon the students in the so-called institutions of higher learning. Many young Southern boys and girls can make it through the former mostly unscathed, but very few make it through the latter intact.

Many a Southerner has become a Confederaphobe and actively persecutes those who openly *express* what he inwardly *represses*. This kind of reconstructed Southerner will typically chronicle his Southern *bone fides* before apologising for slavery, calling his ancestors traitors, and throwing his kith and kin under the proverbial bus. He "knows," and will tell anyone who will listen, that the South is evil, the Confederacy was racist, and that he has now seen the light even though *he* never owned a slave, picked up a gun to fight an invading army, or knew anyone who did! Such a person does violence not only to his people, but to his own soul. They are the worst sort of Confederaphobes because they are what they claim to hate. Confederaphobia eats them from the inside out.

We cannot help who we are, nor should we.

If these Southern tendencies ever begin to re-surface, the self-loathing Southerner is forced to either "come out" or consciously live the Yankee/Nationalist lie. Both paths are scary and fraught with danger.

You can suppress your Southern tendencies, but you can never be a Californian, Bostonian, New Yorker, or a simply an milquetoast American—you can only be a Southerner in denial; a Southerner fighting against his nature; a social experiment; a victim of Stockholm syndrome ... you can try to cover it up, tamp it down, burn it, bury it, have it exorcised, or, if all else fails, give yourself over with reckless abandonment to the American educational establishment, but sooner or later it *will* resurface. Not because it is Southern, but because it is *true*.

CONFEDERAPHOBIA IS THE PROBLEM

BEING A SELF-IDENTIFIED SOUTHERNER is *not* the problem. Being who and what you are is *not* the problem. The Confederate Battle Flag is *not* the problem. Southern people, places, or things currently being targeted and demonized are *not* the problem.

YOU, DEAR SOUTHERN MAN OR WOMAN, ARE <u>NOT</u> THE PROBLEM.

The problem is now, and has long been, one thing and one thing only: CONFEDERAPHOBIA!

Confederaphobes *create* divisiveness and discontent.

Confederaphobes *persecute* and *harass*.

Confederaphobes are the ones *imposing* their views.

Confederaphobes are the ones who *hate*.

Confederaphobes are the ones who *fear* that which they do not understand.

Extract Confederaphobia from the social equation and Confederate displays cease to be "controversial" or "divisive" and people can go on with their lives!

51

Unlike the Confederaphobe, self-identified Southerners have no interest in cultural genocide.

We are content to let the Confederaphobes live their lives as they see fit. <u>We just don't want to be a part of it.</u>

* * *

Why does it matter, folks may ask? Why all the fuss over the dead?

Isn't it time to pull down the flags, demolish the monuments, and plough up the markers? Isn't it time to get with the program? Isn't it time to go along to get along?

O that it were only that simple!

That fact is that our Southern identity, our family and communal ties, and the symbols of the South are all a part of the same interconnected reality in which we live.

Not long ago, a friend of mine,[36] knowing of my interest in the South, asked me if I was a re-enactor. I told her that I was not. She then asked me if I had period clothing. I told her that I did not. I

---

[36] Thank you, KS, for sharing this with me!

proceeded to inquire why she asked. She said a friend of hers was having a family reunion and that they were looking for in re-enactor to read some family "Civil War" letters during the event. I thought it was a neat idea, but she went on to explain that they had tried to read the letters themselves and were unable to do so because of the strong emotions and tears. No one was able to get through them. They needed someone with a little distance to read them.

It is stories like this that help us understand why it is we cling to our history and our heritage. These are not textbooks stories, these are family stories. To strike at the symbols of the South is to strike at those things which are still held sacred and evoke the most tender responses. These are not symbols of ideas, these are reminders of people. Family members. People who we love despite the fact that we have never met.

These symbols are not a matter of ideology, they are not a matter of left or right, *they are personal.*

They remind us that we are a people, not solitary creatures to whom family, faith, and community are incidental or accidental — they are *fundamental* to who and what we are!

They remind us that we did not spring forth *ex nihilo* – out of nothing — but are participants in a larger, unfolding human drama that began before we arrived and, God willing, will continue to unfold in its own unique way long after we are gone.

They remind us that while we are not perfect, we can and must press on — our obligations extend beyond the present. We have a duty to preserve and protect the traditions entrusted to our care and the responsibility to see that they are transmitted to future generations.

They remind us that we are descended from men and women who did not shrink from hardship, nor shirk responsibility when all seemed to be lost—that material ruin and political subjugation did not rob them of their humanity, but made them better appreciate the things that really matter—kith and kin, blood and soil, hearth stones, head stones, and the faith of their fathers.

They teach us that we can and must endure and overcome our own challenges, whatever they may be, with our dignity and honour intact just as they did.

They teach us to be better people. They give us an example to follow.

The sentinels, equestrians, and flags — in many cases at great cost and at great personal sacrifice — were erected to watch over us and help us remember who we are, where we came from, and what we can and should be — both as individuals and as a people.

Most of all — at least today — they remind us that we are a unique and recognizable people that have the right to exist; a right to be who and what we are without molestation, apology, or shame.

We are, of course, more than happy to live and let live and want nothing more than to live in peace with our neighbours and those who may not care for our peculiarities, but we are under no

<u>obligation to participate in our own destruction, or sit quietly while the memory of our kith and kin are slandered and insulted</u>.

Of course, we are perfectly free to do nothing as well—hide in the shadows; stay in the closet; sell our birthright; to go gently into that good night …

That is certainly the path of least resistance, but it is the path of *death* and *destruction*. Not only for us, but for *all people* everywhere who long to be *free*.

Such a thing cannot be if decent people are beaten into submission, forced to live as colonial subjects, or denied their legitimate and lawful right to live openly *as they are* so long as they are willing to permit others to do the same.

In this regard, we are no different than other normal and healthy people. We just happen to do it with a Southern accent.

Coming Out

IF YOU ARE A VICTIM of Confederaphobia, you are not alone. For most people, it takes time to truly come to understand who you are and where you come from.

It's okay to be confused, or to be uncertain about whether (or how) you should come out and live openly and proudly as Southerner; to be who and what you are; to stand tall without apology or shame for your legitimate and praiseworthy history, heritage, and culture.

Education will be a vital part of your recovery as you move from victim to victor.

There are many lies your teachers told you, many falsehoods that need to be addressed. As you become more versed in the true history of the South, your confidence will increase and your fear will decrease.

There are many Southern-friendly resources and organisations out there that can help you along. I will be providing some resources in the appendices.

There is an amazing journey waiting for you should you choose to begin the process of reclaiming your *identity* and, thereby, reclaiming your *life*!

When you are ready to step from the shadows of self-loathing and shame, and embrace your Southern identity, we'll be waiting to receive you with open arms to join us in our struggle as we take our stand against those who insult us because they are insulted, hate us because they accuse us of hate, and deny us our God-given right to exist openly and without fear as a distinct people.

Be brave; be strong; and be true, dear Southerner ...

YOU ARE NOT ALONE!

Appendix A
Recommended Reading

We study history because, as human beings, we have a natural interest in learning about our fellow creatures, even those who lived in different times. Such study can broaden our understanding of human experience and of the workings of human society. It is safe to say that the Confederaphobe does not know anything about history. To him it is merely a few emotionally-charged words. His understanding of human history and human society is juvenile and remarkably ungenerous and inhumane.

This is a shame, because a treasury of great writing about Southern and Confederate history exists, enough for a lifetime of reading and learning.

A few suggestions of starting places for victims of Confederaphobia:

Short works:

The Confederate Catechism by Lyon G. Tyler (son of President John Tyler)

Facts the Historians Leave Out: A Confederate Primer by John S. Tilley

General Histories

North Against South by Ludwell H. Johnson (which should be on the shelf of every Southerner)

To Live and Die in Dixie, edited by Frank Powell

Understanding the War Between the States by Howard R. White and Clyde N. Wilson

The South Was Right! by James R. and Walter D. Kennedy

Shelby Foote's *The Civil War: A Narrative* is an enduring classic of American literature that provides a true portrayal of Confederates.

Important topics

The Real Lincoln by Thomas DiLorenzo

War Crimes Against Southern Civilians by Walter Brian Cisco

Black Confederates by Charles K. Barrow and J.H. Segars

Emancipation Hell by Kirkpatrick Sale

Biographies:

Jefferson Davis: Unconquerable Heart by Elizabeth Allen

R.E. Lee by Douglas S. Freeman

First with the Most: Nathan Bedford Forrest by Robert S. Henry

The websites *AbbevilleInstitute.org* and *SouthernHistorians.org* give access to a wealth of interesting and reliable material about the South. You can download a free copy of *Understanding the War Between the States* (listed above) at *SouthernHistorians.org* and I urge you to do so. More can be found on the Abbeville Institute in Appendix B.

Shotwell Publishing will soon be publishing three small volumes of recommended readings by Dr. Clyde N. Wilson. The "50 Essential Books" series will include a volume on the Antebellum South, The War for Southern Independence, and The New South. Keep an eye out for them. (You can sign-up for new release notifications at *ShotwellPublishing.com*.)

Appendix B
Lectures

If you don't have the time or disposition to do a lot of reading, the Abbeville Institute has some very fine lectures, all of which are available in audio format, some of which are also available in video format—ALL FREE!

You could go to college for 20 years and never even come close to attaining the level of exposure you can get with these lectures alone. I have listened to every single one of these lectures, many of them multiple times. They have opened whole new avenues of study and way of thinking about the cultural heritage and history of the South.

Here's a list of the topics currently available:

- On Being Southern in an Age of Radicalism (2017 Summer School, 14 Lectures)

- Nullification: A 21st Century Remedy (2016 Scholars Conference, 6 Lectures)

- The Southern Tradition and the Renewal of America (2016 Summer School, 12 Lectures)

- The Southern Tradition (2015 Summer School, 13 Lectures)

- The War for Southern Independence (2014 Summer School, 14 Lectures)

- Music and the Southern Tradition (2013 Scholars Conference, 8 Lectures)

- Understanding the South and the Southern Tradition (2013 Summer School, 15 Lectures)

- The War Between the States: Other Voices Other Views (2013 Scholars Conference, 10 Lectures)

- The Greatness of Southern Literature III (2012 Summer School, 14 Lectures)

- The South and America's Wars (2011 Scholars Conference, 10 Lectures)

- The Greatness of Southern Literature II (2011 Summer School, 13 Lectures)

- State Nullification Secession and the Human Scale of Political Order (2010 Scholars Conference, 10 Lectures)

- The Greatness of Southern Literature (2010 Summer School, 12 Lectures)

- The Meaning and Legacy of Reconstruction (2009 Summer School, 17 Lectures)

- Northern Anti-Slavery Rhetoric (2008 Summer School, 13 Lectures)

- The Origin of Southern Identity and the Culture of the Old South (2007 Summer School, 10 Lectures)

- The Southern Agrarian Tradition (2006 Summer School, 12 Lectures)

- Re-Thinking Lincoln: The Man, The Myth, The Symbol, The Legacy (2005 Summer School, 13 Lectures)

- The Southern Critique of Centralization and Nationalism: 1798-1861 (2004 Summer School, 12 Lectures)

- The American Decentralist Tradition (2003 Summer School, 16 Lectures)

In addition to the lectures, the Abbeville Institute publishes articles, reviews, & other items of interest five days a week (Monday through Friday) and follows-up with a podcast that reviews the material on the weekend. Dr. Brion McClanahan hosts the podcast.

The site is also the home of the "Clyde Wilson Library" and the "James McClennan Library." The former contains a massive collection of essays and other items produced by the "Godfather of Southern History," Dr. Wilson. The latter is a comprehensive collection of primary documents of historical significance, essential to any honest study of the South.

If you are serious about learning about "what is true and valuable in the Southern tradition," the material available at the Abbeville Institute is not optional, it is *essential*.

The Abbeville Institute's web page can be found at **www.abbevilleinstitute.org**.

APPENDIX C
WEBSITES

The following is a very small selection of websites that I believe are worth visiting. They are not arranged in any particular order.

Abbeville Institute: www.abbevilleinstitute.org

Society of Independent Southern Historians: southernhistorians.org

Sons of Confederate Veterans: www.scv.org

United Daughters of the Confederacy: hqudc.org

Order of the Confederate Rose: confederateroses.org

Military Order of the Stars and Bars: militaryorderofthestarsandbars.org

King Lincoln Archive: archive.lewrockwell.com/orig2/lincoln-arch.html

American Slave Narratives: An Online Anthology:

xroads.virginia.edu/~hyper/wpa/wpahome.html

Dixie Education: www.dixieedu.org

The Cotton Boll Conspiracy: SouthCarolina1670.Wordpress.com

Dixie Heritage: dixieheritage.net (sign-up for newsletter)

Southern Heritage News and Views: shnv.blogspot.com (sign-up for newsletter)

Know Southern History: knowsouthernhistory.net (Appears to be abandoned, but has a wealth of useful material.)

The Confederate Shop: confederateshop.com (The best online Confederate retailer on the 'net!)

ABOUT THE AUTHOR

PAUL C. GRAHAM is a native of Columbia, South Carolina, and holds Bachelor's and Master's Degrees in Philosophy from the University of South Carolina. He is past president of the South Carolina Masonic Research and the former editor of *The Palmetto Partisan*, the official journal of the South Carolina Division of the Sons of Confederate Veterans.

He was a contributing author to *Understanding the War Between the States* (2015), and editor of a collection of accounts from the South Carolina Slave Narratives titled *When the Yankees Come: Former South Carolina Slaves Remember Sherman's Invasion* (2016).

Mr. Graham's writings have appeared in several publications including the *Simms Review*, *The Palmetto Partisan*, the *Transactions of the SC Masonic Research Society*, and the Abbeville Institute's *Blog* and *Review*.

He is the co-founder of Shotwell Publishing, LLC and lives near old Granby, South Carolina, with his beautiful bride of over 20 years, Mrs. Suzette; their dog, Miss Bella; and two cats, Sully and Mr. Jinx.

You can contact Mr. Graham *via* his website **paulcgraham.com**.

AVAILABLE FROM SHOTWELL

Southern Studies

A Legion of Devils: Sherman in South Carolina by Karen Stokes

Annals of the Stupid Party: Republicans Before Trump by Clyde N. Wilson (The Wilson Files 2)

Dismantling the Republic by Jerry C. Brewer

Dixie Rising: Rules for Rebels by James R. Kennedy

Emancipation Hell: The Tragedy Wrought by Lincoln's Emancipation Proclamation by Kirkpatrick Sale

Lies My Teacher Told Me: The True History of the War for Southern Independence by Clyde N. Wilson

Maryland, My Maryland: The Cultural Cleansing of a Small Southern State by Joyce Bennett.

Nullification: Reclaiming Consent of the Governed by Clyde N. Wilson (The Wilson Files 2)

Punished with Poverty: The Suffering South by James R. & Walter D. Kennedy

Segregation: Federal Policy or Racism? by John Chodes.

Southern Independence. Why War? — The War to Prevent Southern Independence by Dr. Charles T. Pace

Southerner, Take Your Stand! by John Vinson

Washington's KKK: The Union League During Southern Reconstruction by John Chodes.

When the Yankees Come: Former South Carolina Slaves Remember Sherman's Invasion. Edited with Introduction by Paul C. Graham

The Yankee Problem: An American Dilemma by Clyde N. Wilson (The Wilson Files 1)

Fiction

Green Altar Books
Shotwell's Literary Imprint

A New England Romance & Other SOUTHERN Stories by Randall Ivey

Tiller (Clay Bank County, IV) by James Everett Kibler

Gold-Bug Mysteries
Mystery & Thriller Imprint

To Jekyll and Hide by Martin L. Wilson

PUBLISHER'S NOTE

IF YOU ENJOYED THIS BOOK or found it useful, interesting, or informative, we'd be very grateful if you would post a brief review of it on the retailer's website.

In the current political and cultural climate, it is important that we get accurate, Southern-friendly material into the hands of our friends and neighbours. *Your support can really make a difference* in helping us unapologetically celebrate and defend our Southern heritage, culture, history, and home!

———————

For more information, or to sign-up for notification of forthcoming titles, please visit us at

WWW.SHOTWELLPUBLISHING.COM

SHOTWELL
COLUMBIA   So. CAR.
EST. 2015
PUBLISHING

Southern without Apology.

www.ingramcontent.com/pod-product-compliance
Lightning Source LLC
Chambersburg PA
CBHW070022110426
42741CB00034B/2306